A world of faith

A world of faith

WORLD CELEBRATION SPECIAL EDITION

PEGGY FLETCHER STACK & KATHLEEN PETERSON

in partnership with the Interfaith Roundtable
of the Salt Lake Organizing Committee for the
Olympic Winter Games of 2002

SIGNATURE BOOKS

To our children,
who teach us about God.

Thanks to Pat Bagley,
who thought of the idea for this book
and brought us together.

A World of Faith was manufactured in the United States of America
and was printed on acid-free paper.

07   06   05   04   03   02   6   5   4   3   2   1

Library of Congress Cataloging-in-Publication Data is being processed.
Library of Congress control number: 2001 135919

preface

Light the Fire Within.™ This is the theme of the Olympic Winter Games in Salt Lake City. It refers to the inner spark that drives athletes to reach their highest potential. It could also suggest a belief in the divine light that radiates within every human being, an idea that is taught in every religious tradition.

The Olympic ideals, as symbolized by five rings, parallel notions common in spiritual teachings. The first ideal is peace, which can be within one soul or among nations. The second is friendship and goodwill among people. The third is fair play and sportsmanship, which reflect the commitment to justice that is common to all belief systems. The fourth is appreciation of art, which, in many cases throughout history, has glorified the divine. The fifth is brightness and enthusiasm for the Games.

Religious motivation has been part of the Games from the beginning when the competitions were held in a stadium in Olympia, near Athens, to honor the Greek gods and were accompanied by pageantry normally associated with religion—processions, sacrifices, altars, flames, and banquets. Feats of prowess and agility were meant to please Zeus, the chief god, and then Apollo and Poseidon. For the athletes, body and soul were inseparable. To attempt the impossible, they had to ignite an inner fire in the name of a higher power.

Today's athletes drive their bodies to peak performance by uniting spirit and motion. They often thank God, an unnamed Supreme Being, or a superhuman spark for these gifts and accomplishments and feel aided by a power that exceeds their own.

The same impulse that drives physical achievement also creates new civilizations and communities. Whether we call it God, inner light, faith, or revelation, human beings have always sought something better, higher, and more pure.

Every culture the world over has established a set of beliefs about the way the world works and how it responds to a Higher Source. Sometimes those views conflict, even violently. Organized religion has inspired the best in human history: new and often revolutionary social teachings about justice, glorious houses of worship, works of art, and acts of selflessness. It has also spawned the worst depravity, cruelty, forced conversions, and war.

The best hope to end such conflict in the name of religion is increased knowledge of the various traditions and what they have in common. This book celebrates that quest to understand diversity. It is a glimpse, a taste, an awakening.

Each section of this book opens with a story about a particular faith's origins. We talk about founders and founding events in a simplified way. This is not academic history but faith stories told in the words of that tradition. The second paragraph for each tradition conveys some of the current practices, focusing on infancy, coming of age, worship, and marriage rituals.

To verify accuracy and tone, every page has been read by people who represent that faith or by a religion scholar . The language may occasionally seem difficult or "insider" for those not of the faith, but we believe it is important for children from each tradition to recognize themselves and their faith in words that are familiar to them.

The religions are organized in alphabetical order. We omitted mentioning how many adherents a religion has because we believe religious ideas should be considered on their merits and not by the size of the group. We have chosen to illustrate the faiths with images that are largely historical because current believers tend to dress more alike. An understanding of history is crucial to grasp both the differences and similarities among traditions.

The twenty-eight faith groups are representative. We chose Hopi to convey the sense of the Native American religions, although there are wide differences among the more than 500 Indian traditions. In Utah, for example, there are five major tribes:

Goshute, Navajo, Paiute, Shoshoni, and Ute. Similarly, Yorubas stand for all African tribal religions, of which there are hundreds. Because America's religious landscape is dominated by Christians, we describe more Christian variations than other religions. But we are well aware that there are dozens more Protestant groups as well as many sects of Buddhism, Hinduism, Islam, and Judaism that we could have portrayed.

To reduce redundancy, we have not described the story of Jesus common to all Christian believers. Christians see Jesus as the Christ, the Son of God, who became a man 2,000 years ago. According to the Christian Bible, Jesus was put to death on a cross, but then rose from the dead. Christians believe that by accepting Jesus as Christ, they will be forgiven for their sins and live with God forever. This book emphasizes the ways in which each Christian group's understanding or emphasis is a bit different from all the others.

Bigotry begins with ignorance. Many people know little or nothing about faiths other than their own. Worse, some believers demonize those of other faiths, completely misunderstanding the essence of that belief system, mistaking politics for doctrines.

The Olympic Winter Games provide a chance for global understanding. We hope these pages will show people of the 21st century their connectedness so that they can be tomorrow's peacemakers. Our world needs them more than ever.

Peggy Fletcher Stack and Kathleen Peterson
November 2001

vii

greeting

As we prepare to help welcome the world to the 2002 Olympic Winter Games, we see an opportunity to increase appreciation for the diversity and beauty of the global human family. These competitions bring together people from diverse nations, races, and religions. It is a time to celebrate the excellence of the human spirit through its physical manifestations. It is a time of international truce when people put aside their differences and celebrate the victories of individual striving.

Given the world shaking tragedies of September 11, 2001, the subsequent blame and persecution of innocent people of Middle Eastern descent and of the Muslim faith, and the ensuing battles overseas, we feel the message of faith, unity, and love is ever more urgent. Indeed, even before the September terrorist attacks, religion had already emerged as a potentially divisive issue in the 2002 Olympic Winter Games. Some had called these "the Mormon Olympics." It is true that Salt Lake City was founded by Mormons escaping religious persecution and that it is still the world headquarters of the Church of Jesus Christ of Latter-day Saints. However, this is also a city where, in the year 2001, about 50 percent of the population belong to other faiths. All of the religious communities together add to the beauty and culture of the city.

As a sub-committee of the Salt Lake Organizing Committee, we felt a need to acknowledge the faiths here and around the globe that will come together for this event and that otherwise enrich our world culture. Representatives of all faiths were invited to form our roundtable in 1998. Since that time, we have worked together to develop greater understanding, respect, and collaboration. In doing so, we have grown closer as a community. The following are some of our accomplishments.

We invited the local community to participate in what we hope to be an annual event of music and blessing called "An Interfaith Tribute to the Human Spirit." We prepared a directory of faith communities to be made available at the airport, hotels, and information booths throughout the city. We helped arrange for more than 700 host homes for athletes' families. We developed a website that features the histories of religious communities in Utah, with a link to each faith's website. Together with other groups, we supported the renovation of the Fort Douglas Post Chapel, built in 1883—the second oldest military chapel in the nation—as an Interfaith Chapel and center for the Olympic Village. We hope it will remain a permanent fixture of Utah's religious community long into the future. We coordinated the Chaplains Program for the Olympic Village and Paralympic Village.

With this book, the Interfaith Roundtable hopes to leave another legacy to the world community: increased understanding, appreciation, and respect for all the world's religious traditions. The beautiful illustrations and text, as well as the book's emphasis on the Golden Rule found in all religions, give a glimpse of the beauty and goodness of the world's faiths and should spark a greater desire in readers to pursue more awareness of cultural diversity.

The Olympic Winter Games are an opportunity to experience the global community in a context of peace. We hope this book will help readers find an increased desire to build a more peace-filled society.

Interfaith Roundtable

General Council of the Assemblies of God
Rev. Dean L. Jackson

Calvary Baptist Church
Rev. France Davis

Baha'i Faith
Jan Saeed (chair, Interfaith Roundtable)

First Baptist Church
Rev. Clarice Duke

Southern Baptist Church
Beth Ann Williams

Brigham Young University
Dr. Roger Keller

Salt Lake Buddhist Temple
Rev. Jerry Hirano

Zen Buddhist
Jamie Chandler

Roman Catholic
Diocese of Salt Lake City, Utah
Sister Bridget Clare McKeever,
Michael Lee, and Monica Howa-Johnson

Japanese Church of Christ
Laurie Sakaeda

Christian Center of Park City
Tim Dahlin

Christian Science
Nancy Garland, Trinka Wasik, Emma Allen,
Karen Gauthier, and Sabrina Stillwell

Coalition of Religious Communities
Linda Hilton

Community Churches in Utah
Nancy Kruse

First Congregational Church of Salt Lake
Rev. Art Ritter and Viva Baldwin

St. Luke's Episcopal Church, Park City
Rev. Patrick Finn

St. Paul's Episcopal Church
Rev. Ivan Cendese and Rev. Caryl Marsh

Interfaith Peace Making
Resource Center of Utah
Bruce Kaliser

Park City Interfaith
Paddy Hiss-Wood

Islamic Society of Greater Salt Lake
Dr. Iqbal Hossain and Masood Ul-Hasan

Congregation Kol Ami
Rabbi Frederick Wenger

Lutheran Churches
Chaplain Bob Schrank, FBI

Christ Lutheran, LCMS, Murray
Nina Brollier

Mt. Tabor Lutheran Church
Rev. Steve Leiser

Our Savior's Lutheran
Reba Kiger and Rev. Roger Anderson

Shepherd of the Mountains
Lutheran, Park City
Jeffrey Louden

Church of Jesus Christ of Latter-day Saints
Ray Beckham, Janette Hales Beckham,
Sheldon F. Child, and Steve Kohlert

Salt Lake Organizing Committee
William Shaw, Wayne Saltzgiver,
Julie Groves, and Alan Barnes

Presbytery of Utah
Marvin Groote, executive presbyter

Primary Children's Medical Center
Chaplain Michael Jackson

Religious Society of Friends (Quakers),
Salt Lake Monthly Meeting
Elaine C. Emmi

Salt Lake Reformed Christians Church
John Jonkman and Thomas Vander Ziel

The Salvation Army
Maj. Wayne Froderberg, Patty Warren,
and Daniel Williams

Seventh-Day Adventist Church, Central
Pastor Roland Nwosu

Unitarian Universalist
Rev. Silvia Behrend and Rev. Tom Goldsmith

Holladay United Church of Christ
Pastor Richard Waddell

United Methodist
Rev. Ronald Hodges, Rev. Scott Schiesswohl,
Cynthia Schiesswohl, George Everett,
and Diana Stockebrand

United Methodist
Peace with Justice Committee
Annie Heart

University of Utah Hospital
Chaplain Mark Allison

Utah Women in Ministry
Maxine Hanks

WHALE Center
Rev. Dr. David W. Randle

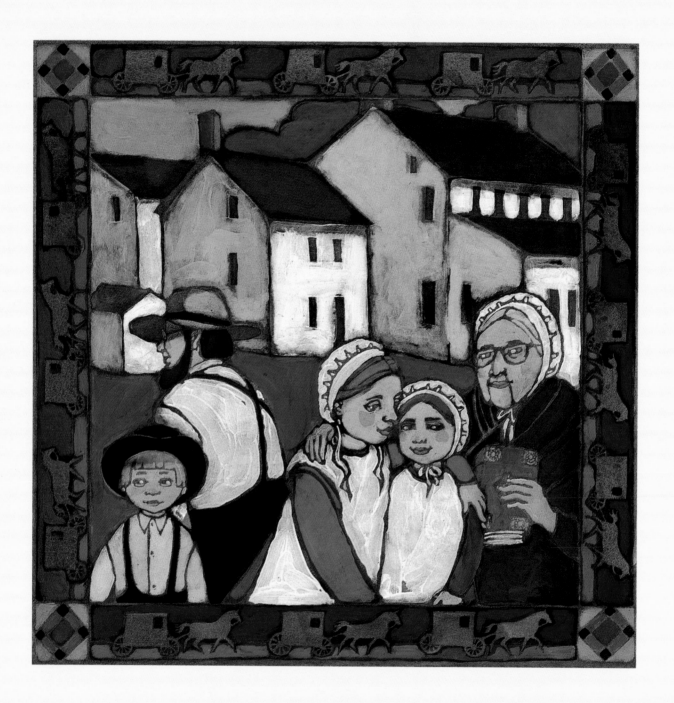

Amish

In 1694 Jacob Ammann, a Swiss farmer, liked things to be plain and simple. He wanted to live like Jesus. Ammann and his followers—who became known as the "Amish"—hated big houses and fancy clothes. When people all around them were fighting, they refused to get involved. At the end of the Thirty Years' War between Protestants and Catholics in Europe, each prince was allowed to choose the religion for everyone in his territory. Because the Amish would not join any other church, they were forced from their homes and punished. They escaped to America, where they settled in Pennsylvania.

Amish men and women still dress like people of long ago. The men have beards and wear broad-brimmed black hats. The women wear long, plain dresses and white bonnets. They live on farms with no electricity, telephones, or cars because they believe that modern conveniences distract them from God. Church services—which may last up to three hours—are held every other week in a home. Men take turns being minister. Twice a year the congregation gathers for foot-washing—men to men, women to women—following Jesus' example at the Last Supper. They take joy in obeying the rules of God in families and communities, untouched by the worries of the world.

Illustration: Typical homes used for meetings; horse-drawn buggies; a quilting block.

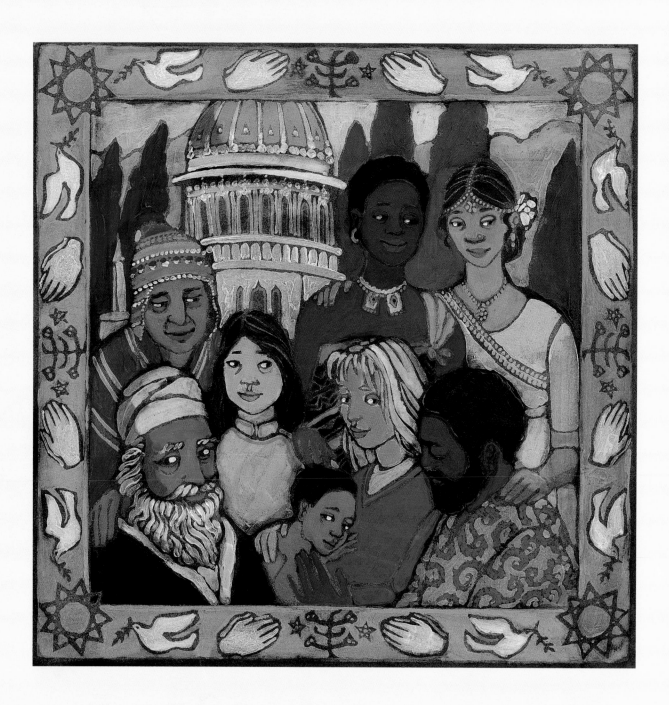

Baha'is

In 1844 a man called the Bab, which means "gate," announced to the people of Persia (now Iran) that a messenger of God was coming soon. The Bab said that this new prophet would bring peace to all the world. But the people were afraid of the Bab. They thought he was rebelling against the government, so they killed him. A few years later a young man came forward to say that he was the messenger that the Bab had foretold. The young man was called Baha'u'llah, or "Glory of God." He taught the people that God had sent many prophets to this world at different times. God is one, he said, and all religions have truth. The peoples of the earth are like differently colored flowers in a beautiful garden. Baha'u'llah was tortured and imprisoned for his beliefs.

Baha'is revere Baha'u'llah as the divine teacher for this day. They have no priests or clergy, but each group is led by a nine-member spiritual assembly. They pray three times a day. Every nineteen days they hold a feast to pray, study, enjoy each other's company, and remember events in their history. Baha'i children study world religions and Baha'i houses of worship have nine sides and nine doors to symbolize the many paths to God, who is continuously revealed to humanity. But most of all, Baha'is teach world peace and unity through understanding and obedience to the laws of God.

Illustration: The Shrine of the Bab at Mt. Carmel, Haifa, Israel; hands symbolize prayer; the dove means peace; the nine-pointed star represents the unity of all religions; the three-tiered symbol represents God, the holy messengers, and humanity.

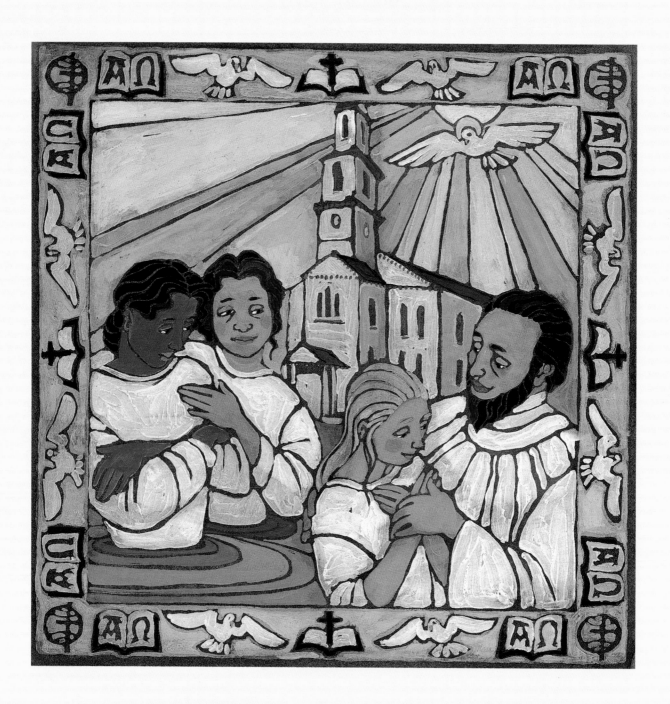

Baptists

Roger Williams was an independent Englishman who insisted on worshipping God in his own way. He sailed to America in 1631 to get away from the state-sponsored religion in England. He expected more religious freedom in America, but when he arrived in Massachusetts, the Puritans had established an official church and demanded strict obedience to it. When Williams complained to the leaders, saying that people should be able to follow their own conscience, they forced him to leave. He fled into the wilderness during the coldest snows of winter. Finally, Williams settled in Rhode Island and declared that in this colony people would be allowed to choose their own religion. His was the first Baptist church in America.

Baptists reject the idea of infant baptisms, saying that people must understand Christ's teachings before they can be baptized. They also teach that during baptism a person should be fully immersed in water. Today's Baptists celebrate the Lord's Supper at least four times a year. They revere the Bible as the inspired word of God. Each Baptist church is independent of all the other ones, though some churches unite for common missions. Baptists have a passion for "soul freedom" or choosing their own faith and actions.

Illustration: First Baptist church, built in 1774 in Providence, Rhode Island; Hebrew letters on the book are alpha and omega, the beginning and the end; the dove means the Holy Spirit; in the corner is the symbol of American Baptists.

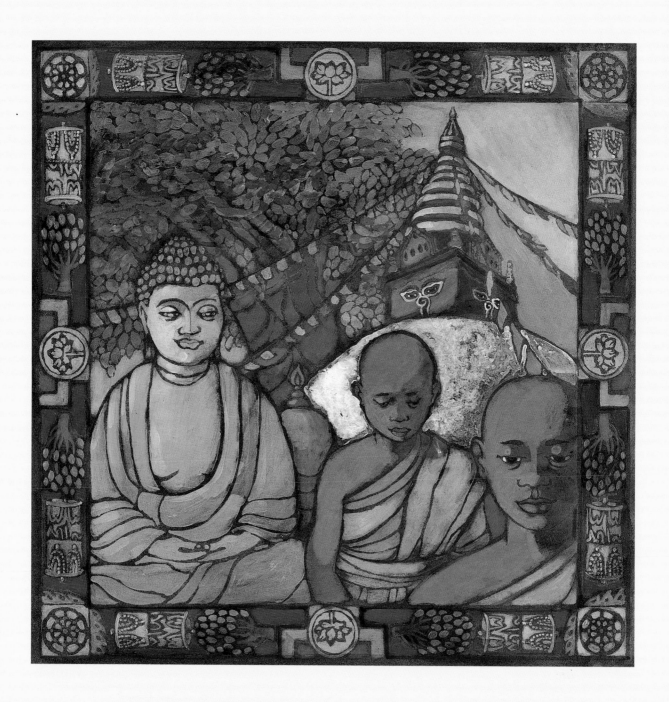

Buddhists

In about 536 B.C. Siddhartha Gautama, a prince in India, left his home in search of wisdom. He spent six years living in a forest and listening to religious teachers. But he was not satisfied. Finally one day he sat under a bodhi tree and decided to stay until he received some answers. By morning, his mind was opened to a vision of life's deeper meaning and to his previous lives. According to tradition, that was the day Siddhartha became the Buddha, which means "the enlightened one."

Life is mostly suffering that comes from wanting things, says the Buddha. These desires can be overcome by following an eight-fold path called the Middle Way, which avoids all extremes. Buddhists believe in treating all living things with respect, speaking honestly, helping others, and learning to focus the mind. Those who follow this path will understand the truths of the universe. They believe there is no individual soul or self. Instead, people are reincarnated, or born at different times, again and again until they reach Nirvana, or perfect harmony with all things, and are freed from the cycle. In some parts of Asia, Buddhist men and women become nuns and monks who wear simple orange robes, eat only one meal a day, live together in communities, and never marry. All Buddhists seek enlightenment like Buddha.

Illustration: The Bodhnath Stupa in Kathmandu, Nepal; a prayer wheel, bodhi tree, and lotus flower, which symbolize remaining clean in a muddy pond. The wheel of truth in the corner has eight spokes representing the eight-fold path.

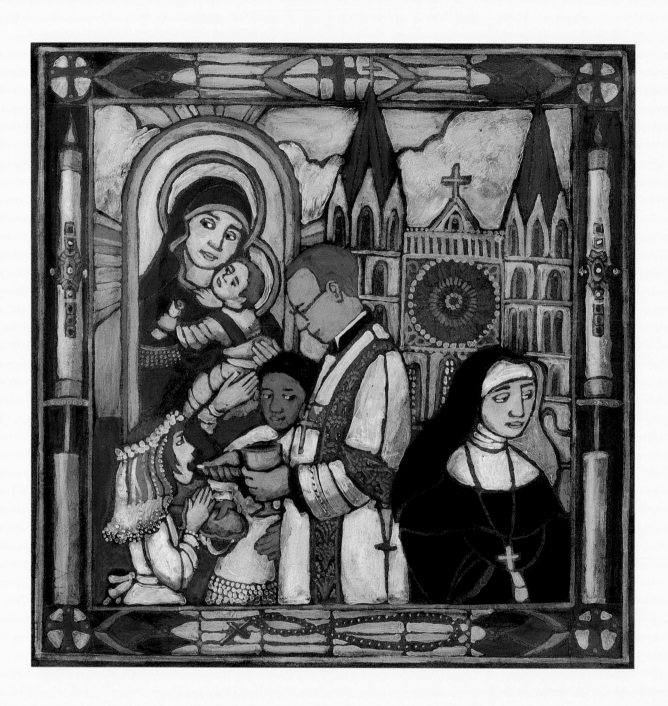

catholics

In the Bible it says that Jesus of Nazareth could heal the sick and raise the dead. People followed him everywhere to hear his teachings. During his ministry, Jesus chose twelve followers to be his apostles. One of them, a fisherman named Peter, became the leader of the apostles. For Roman Catholics, Peter was the first pope. Throughout the ages, popes and other church leaders have explained Jesus' life and teachings and spread the good news of the Christian gospel.

Catholics believe the word of God is found in the Bible and in church teachings and practices. Special ceremonies called sacraments are at the heart of Catholic life and are ways in which God's saving love is expressed through the church. Some sacraments are celebrated at important moments like birth, becoming mature, marriage, and death. Other sacraments such as confessing of sins and participating in the Mass (commemorating the Lord's Supper) occur more often. In the Mass, Catholics believe the bread and wine are mysteriously transformed into the body and blood of Christ. Catholics revere Jesus' mother, Mary, as both a saint and the Mother of God. Saints are people who were especially close to God in this life; from heaven they help the living. Priests and nuns are men and women who remain single in order to better serve God and the church. For Catholics, God is present and active in every experience of life.

Illustration: Chartres Cathedral in France; a young girl's first Communion; the cross is a symbol of the crucifixion of Jesus Christ; rosary beads are used to help with prayers; a pascal candle is used especially at Easter.

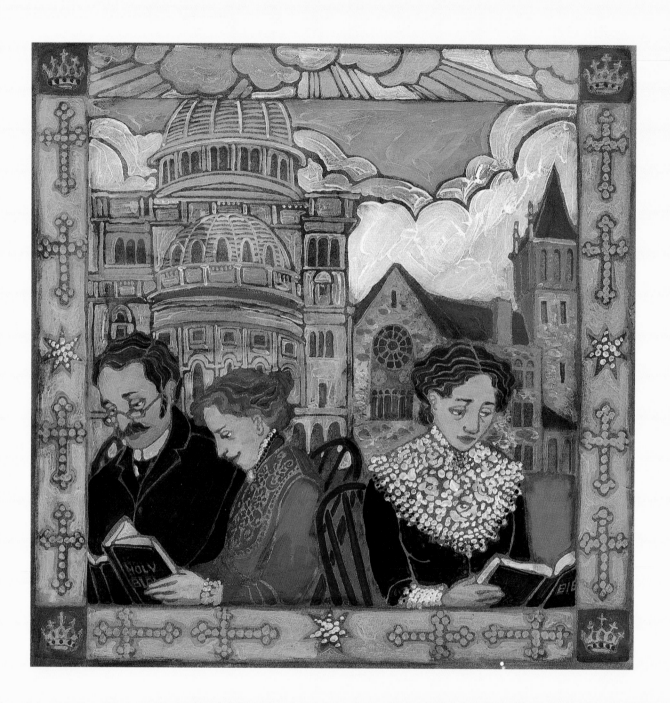

christian scientists

As a child in the 1830s, Mary Baker Eddy was constantly sick. She took lots of medicines and talked with many doctors but nothing made her well. Mary slipped on some ice in 1866 and was told she would never walk again. In desperation, she turned to the Bible for help. She carefully read the stories about Jesus healing people. She thought and prayed about it and, suddenly, was healed. Then she began an intensive three-year study of the Bible. In the sacred book, Eddy discovered a clear, scientific method of Christian healing. Seven years later, she published *Science and Health with a Key to the Scriptures* and founded the Church of Christ, Scientist, in Boston, Massachusetts.

God is Life, Truth, and Love, Eddy taught. Suffering, including physical pain and death, is an illusion. As soon as people grasp this, they can be healed. Approved Christian Science "practitioners" are special members who help sick people understand their illnesses and get rid of them. Heaven is not a place but is being in harmony with God. At services, worshippers read passages from the Bible and Eddy's book. Once a week members share testimonies of healings. The church is known for its highly respected newspaper, *The Christian Science Monitor*, and its reading rooms where people can study scripture, pray, or experience the goodness of God.

Illustration: The Mother Church and Original Church in Boston, Massachusetts; sun rays and clouds represent divine healing; the cross and crown are the symbols of Christ Science; the woman in the lower right is Mary Baker Eddy.

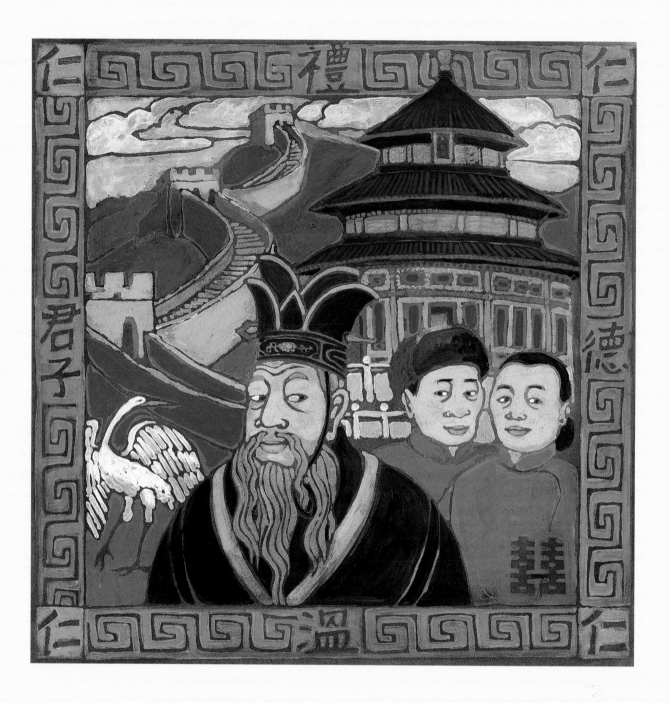

confucianism

Confucius was a Chinese gentleman, born around 500 B.C., who felt that the people of his time had forgotten the way to behave. Local rulers fought with each other, being greedy and creating chaos. Confucius studied great teachings from the past, then traveled the countryside sharing his ideas. He taught people to be kind to their neighbors, to honor their parents, respect their leaders, and hold their tempers. He said that everyone, rich and poor, should be educated in the arts. His ideas, though simple, had a powerful effect on people in China. Soon he had many followers who compiled his teachings into books to be studied and memorized. After Confucius died, people built temples to honor him and required all government workers to pass a test on his teachings.

Today in China, many study Confucianism, learning the basics of good behavior and thinking. They visit his temples, which honor the wise man he was but which also revere several teachers of Confucianism who came after him. Their religious ceremonies include animal sacrifices as well as elaborate dances and music. They celebrate a boy's entrance into manhood or a girl's engagement to be married. On both occasions, the young candidate is given new clothes and a new name as a grown-up. But most of all, Confucianism is reflected in the everyday thinking of the people of China.

Illustration: T'ien T'an (part of the Temple of Heaven in Peking, China, built in 1420); the crane is a symbol of strength and longevity; the border letters symbolize the teachings of Confucius.

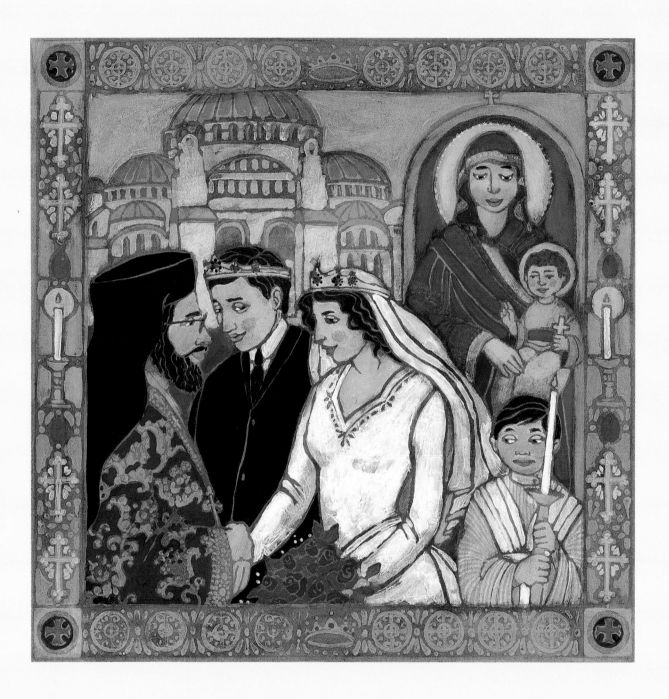

Eastern Orthodox

On the eve of an important battle for control of the Roman Empire in 312 A.D., Constantine the Great saw a flaming cross symbolizing Jesus Christ in the sky and the words, "With this sign, conquer." After his victory, Constantine converted to Christianity, making it the empire's official religion. He moved the capital eastward to Constantinople (today's Istanbul in Turkey). Christians in the Eastern Roman Empire argued with those in the West over the exact relationship of God, Jesus, and the Holy Spirit. They also disagreed about whether the pope was the supreme head of the church or just one bishop among many. Language also divided them: people in the east spoke Greek; those in the west used Latin. By 1054 a split in the church was unavoidable. Those in the east became the Eastern Orthodox and those in the west were known as Roman Catholics. This split is known as "the Great Schism."

The Eastern Orthodox church, which is organized by regions such as Greek Orthodox or Russian Orthodox, shares many beliefs and practices with the Roman Catholic church including ceremonies known as sacraments. But in the Orthodox church, infants are baptized by immersion and some priests can marry. In the church's colorful marriage ceremony, the bride and groom wear crowns symbolizing their new joy in marriage and Christ. Orthodox services use icons, or paintings of figures and saints from the Bible, to help them express their love of God. It is a faith steeped in mystery and beauty.

Illustration: The Hagia Sophia in Istanbul, Turkey; candles symbolize the light of Christ's gospel; the crown symbolizes the triumph of Jesus over death.

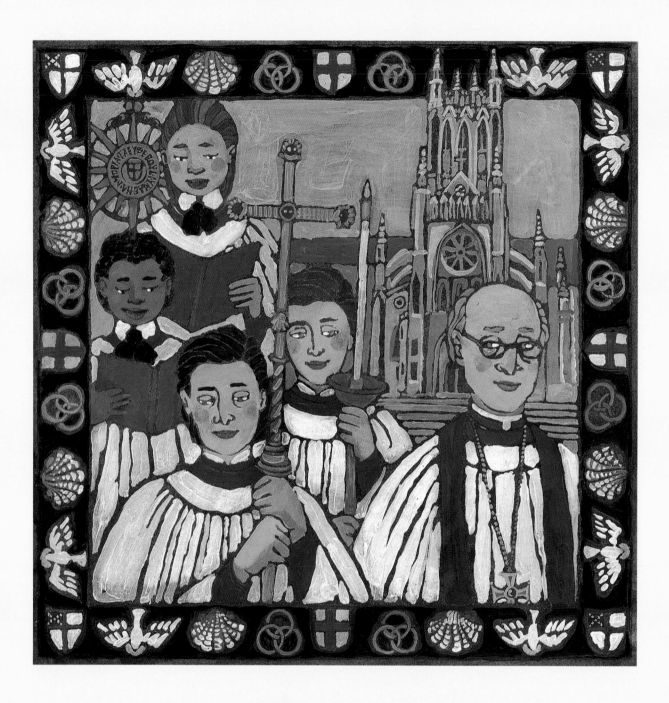

Episcopalians

Legend has it that Joseph of Arimathea, the man who provided a tomb for Jesus, traveled to England and planted a sprig from Christ's crown of thorns. The thorn tree slowly flowered there, so the story goes, and so did Christianity. By the 16th century, tensions between King Henry VIII of England and the Catholic pope boiled over. They argued about marriage laws, church property, and who would govern the church. Finally Henry said that from then on, British kings and queens would be the "Supreme Head" of the Church of England, even choosing its bishops. At the end of the American Revolution, the colonists from England established their own bishops. While maintaining ties to England, American members eventually became known as Episcopalians, from the Greek word "episkopos," meaning bishop.

Episcopalians worship God with magnificent music, reverence, and awe. Their British ancestors built stately cathedrals and produced two of the most majestic books in the English language: the King James translation of the Bible and the *Book of Common Prayer*, which contains readings still used in services. Like Catholics, Lutherans, and Eastern Orthodox, Episcopalians believe in Christ's real presence at the Lord's Supper. They baptize infants and adults by pouring, sprinkling, or immersing them into water. The Episcopal church is still connected to the Church of England, which has branches on every continent. Together the churches form the Anglican Communion, which tries to follow Christ in his suffering, forgiveness and compassion.

Illustration: The National Cathedral in Washington, D.C.; the compass rose is the symbol of the Anglican Communion; the Episcopal shield represents the old church and new church; the clamshell symbolizes baptism; gold rings suggest the Trinity.

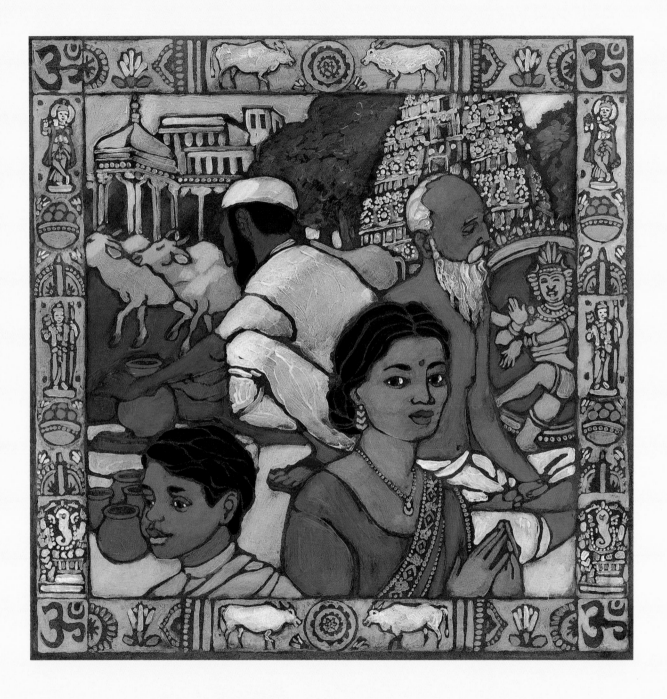

Hindus

Over three thousand years ago, a wandering Aryan tribe settled on the banks of the Indus River (in modern-day India) and told stories of many gods. They spoke of Vishnu, a God who comes to earth in different forms to help people. Once he was a giant fish who warned of a coming flood. Another time he was a prince named Rama, who had to battle demons to rescue his kidnapped wife. He also came as Krishna, a chariot driver who helped the chief warrior do his duty in battle. All these gods were part of Brahman, the spirit of the universe, and knowledge of them was passed down in sacred writings known as Vedas.

Like Buddhists, Hindus believe that human souls are born over and over into different circumstances until they reach perfection or union with God. For Hindus, every action has a consequence in this life or the next. This is called the law of karma. Bad actions could lead to a new life full of suffering; good choices may be rewarded with good fortune. Most Hindu homes have a family shrine where the faithful light a lamp and pray every day. They often leave fruit, flowers, and food at the shrine to be blessed by the gods. Because cows and other animals are revered as sacred, some Hindus will not eat meat. Hindu worship and disciplined meditation open their minds and hearts to God.

Illustration: Rajgopuram, the Hindu Temple of Greater Chicago; the word "OM" expresses the complete nature of God; the gods Krishna, Rama, and Ganesh are in the border; fruit, incense, and candles are offerings to the gods; cows represent four paths to union with God.

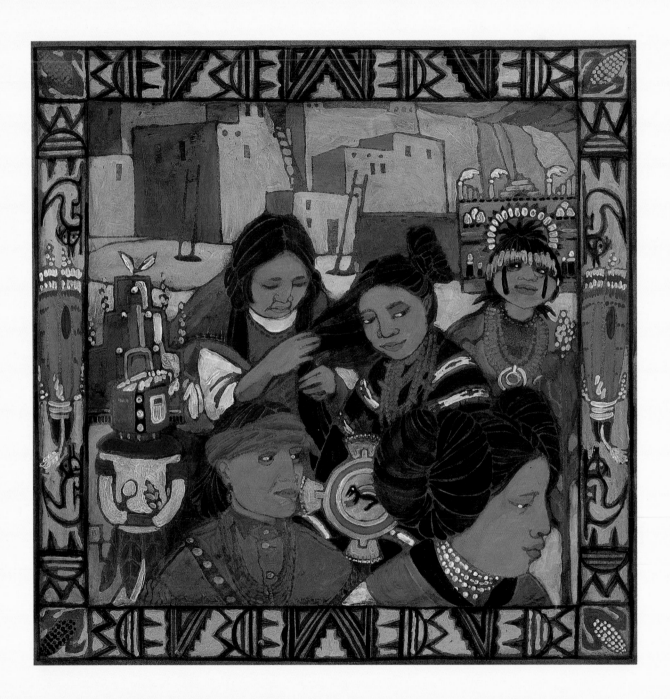

HOPIS

In the beginning, say the Hopis, human beings lived underground, far below the surface of the earth. But they were crowded and constantly tripping over each other. So they made their way up through three different worlds until they found a hole in the earth's surface. They climbed through the hole to see the sky and breathe the air. This was the Fourth World. God told the humans that this world is not as easy as the other three. It has height and depth, heat and cold, beauty and emptiness. Humans must choose the good, God said, and carry out the plan of creation. Then God left them, with only spirits or "kachinas" to guide them on their journey.

Hopis are among the Pueblo Indians of the American West. They hold ceremonies in underground chambers called "kivas." A small hole in the corner represents the place humans entered the world. To Hopis, corn is a symbol of life. When Hopi babies are born, they are given a special blanket and a perfect ear of corn. Kachinas—ancestral spirits—bring rain, heal the sick, and help crops grow. Every season dancers dressed as kachinas, with painted bodies and colorful masks, use lively rituals to call on the spirits. Hopis celebrate all of God's creations and try to keep harmony in the universe.

Illustration: A Hopi pueblo in Mesa Verde, Colorado; the four colors of corn—red, black, yellow, and white—represent brotherhood; the eagle feathers symbolize power; kachinas are intermediaries between people and gods.

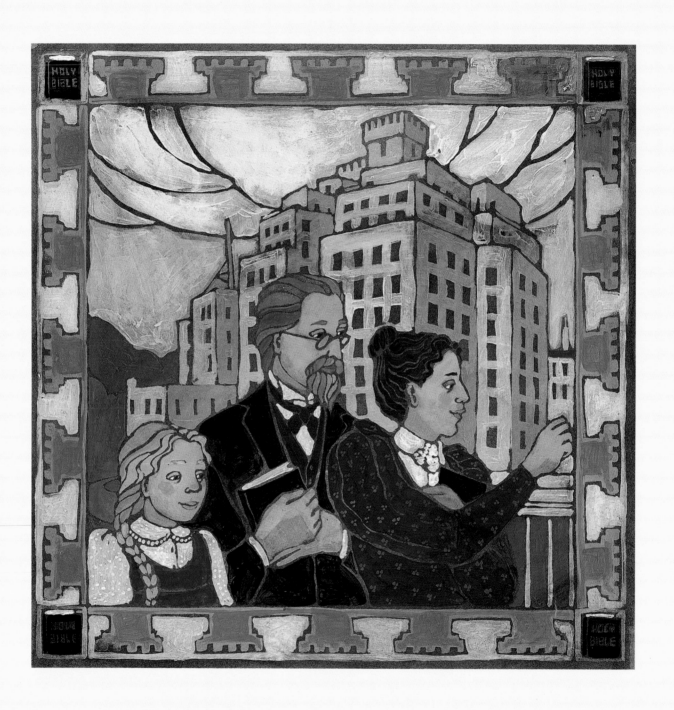

Jehovah's witnesses

The late 1880s were tough times in America. Workers were fighting with their bosses, people were getting poorer, and the world was getting ready for war. Charles Taze Russell was convinced that Jesus was coming soon. He believed that there would be a big battle in which the wicked would be destroyed forever and the righteous would rule the world for 1,000 years. By 1931, many people agreed with him. They established the Watch Tower Bible and Tract Society in Brooklyn, New York, and called themselves Jehovah's Witnesses. Witnesses were often persecuted for their devotion to God above country and for their refusal to salute flags or serve in the military. In America they eventually won the right to practice their religion in their own way.

Witnesses believe that God—known as Jehovah, a name derived from Hebrew—once existed alone. Jesus was Jehovah's first creation as a spirit son. He was born a man and then became man's savior by his perfect obedience. Every Jehovah's Witness endeavors to preach the faith's message through the church magazine, *The Watchtower*, at least ten hours a month. Witnesses don't celebrate Christmas or Easter. Instead, they commemorate what they believe is the biblical anniversary of Christ's death. Baptism is their only other religious ceremony. They believe faithfully in Christ's return.

Illustration: World Headquarters in Brooklyn, New York; the watchtower symbolizes the need to watch for the return of Jesus; every member is a missionary.

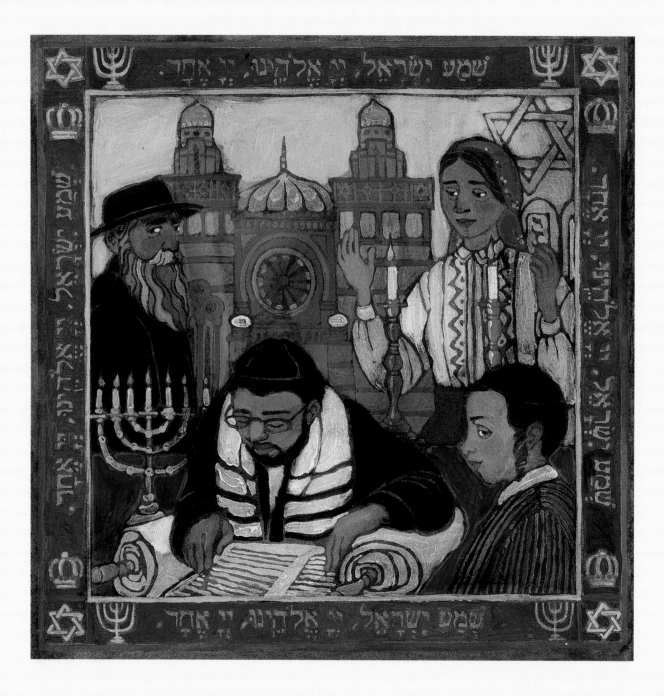

Jews

In the ancient land of Canaan near the Mediterranean Sea lived a man named Abraham. He was a good and noble man who believed in one God. But his neighbors worshipped many gods, even gods made of bronze. Abraham's God made a promise to him. If he worshipped only God and obeyed God's rules, he would bless Abraham and all his children for many generations to come. God would give them a special land and protection from their enemies. Jews get their name from Judah, a great-grandson of Abraham.

Jews read, study, and revere the words of their ancient prophets and leaders which are written in the Torah—the first five books of the Bible. The Torah sets out the rules and practices of a righteous life, including the Ten Commandments. Jews observe a weekly day of rest, or sabbath, from sundown Friday until sundown Saturday. When Jewish boys are thirteen, they read from the Torah in Hebrew at a synagogue service called a "bar mitzvah." By doing this, they become members of the congregation. In some groups girls have the same ceremony, called a "bat mitzvah." Jews celebrate God's past and present miracles with holidays throughout the year. And they strive to be faithful to Abraham's promises to God.

Illustration: Bouwneesterstraat Synagogue in Antwerp, Belgium; the Star of David; the menorah, the oldest symbol of Judaism; the writing says, "Hear, O Israel, the Lord is our God, the Lord is one."

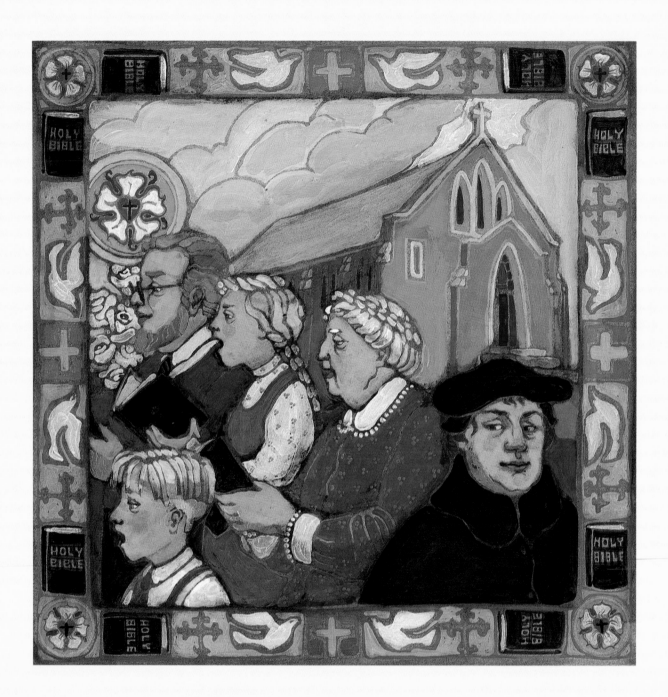

Lutherans

As a Catholic monk in sixteenth-century Germany, Martin Luther spent a lot of time wondering if he was pleasing God. He was frustrated with his own failure to be holy. He was also troubled by some of the church's practices. Could people buy their way out of hell as the church was then teaching? No, Luther decided, these practices were wrong. He made a list of 95 complaints and nailed them to a castle door in Wittenberg. Though Luther only meant to reform the Catholic church, his actions launched the Protestant Reformation and divided Christians into many different groups.

People do not need priests to understand the Bible, Luther taught; they can study it themselves. To make it easier for common folk, he translated the Bible from Latin into German. All believers are priests, he said. But no matter how hard people try to be good, everyone sins. Only faith in Jesus Christ and repentance will lead a person to heaven. Holy lives are built upon faith, not actions. Lutherans baptize infants by sprinkling or pouring water onto their foreheads. They celebrate the Lord's Supper each week, believing—like Catholics, Episcopalians, and Eastern Orthodox—that Christ is truly present in the bread and wine. And once a year on Reformation Sunday, Lutherans remember the grace-filled courage of their founder.

Illustration: St. John's Evangelical Lutheran church; Martin Luther's coat of arms; the Luther rose: the Christian heart rests on roses beneath the cross, the dove means the Holy Spirit; Luther is in the lower right-hand corner.

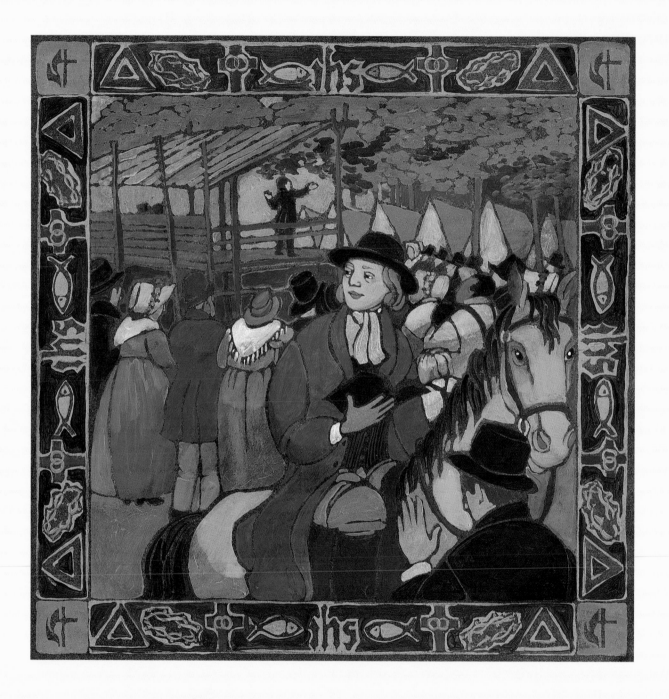

Methodists

John Wesley, an eighteenth-century priest in the Church of England, believed it was possible to be perfect. He planned every minute of his time to study, pray, or discuss religious ideas. Wesley's fellow students called him and his friends "Methodists" because they were so methodical or orderly. Years later Wesley had a sudden, inner feeling that Christ loved him. He started preaching in open fields. His brother Charles wrote more than 6,000 hymns to be sung during these outdoor meetings. During the American Revolution, Methodist societies in the United States broke off from the Church of England and formed a church of their own. On the western frontier, every Methodist minster was a "circuit-rider," traveling from place to place, holding services in large tents, preaching to thousands day and night.

Methodists still strive for perfection. They want to make the world a better place and they believe God is helping them, encouraging them, and showing the way. Like Catholics, they baptize infants. For Methodists, the Bible is the inspired word of God and all people must read and understand it for themselves. Methodists celebrate the Lord's Supper often. And they love the joyous singing of hymns—many composed by Charles Wesley.

Illustration: A typical camp meeting and circuit rider; the cross and flame symbolize zeal to preach the gospel; the triangle suggests the Trinity; the cross and rings represent marriage; the fish is the symbol of Jesus Christ; IHS means Jesus in Greek.

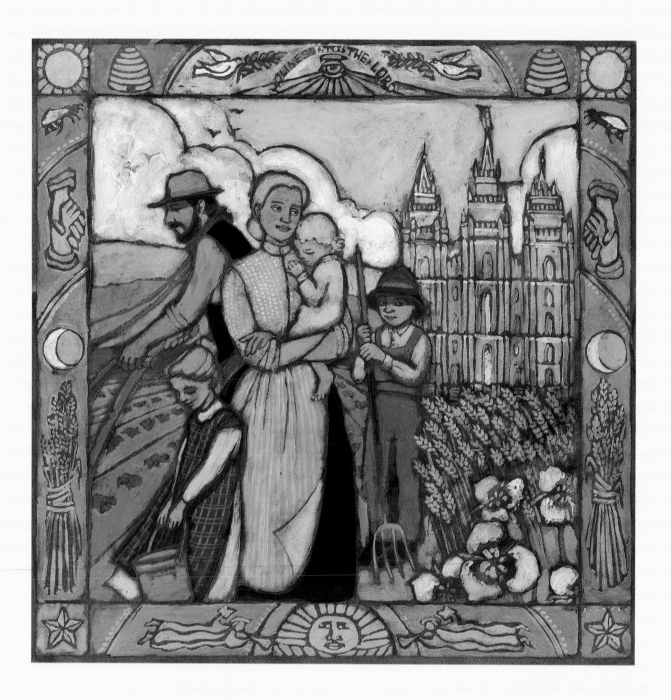

Mormons

In 1820 a fourteen-year-old New York farm boy, Joseph Smith Jr., told his family and neighbors he had a vision of God and Jesus Christ while praying in a grove of trees. These other-worldly visitors told him that precious truths of Christianity had been lost but would be restored. Some years later, Joseph was led by an angel to golden plates buried in the ground. The plates told the story of Christ's visit to a group of ancient Israelites who had sailed to the Americas. With God's help, Smith translated the record called the Book of Mormon. Mormons believe it is scripture, along with the Bible. Smith founded The Church of Jesus Christ of Latter-day Saints in 1830, but many other Christians believed that Mormons were wrong. They drove Mormons from state to state until Smith was killed by a mob in 1844. Brigham Young, who became the church's next president, led the Mormons to the mountains of Utah where they established a close-knit community.

Mormons follow some traditional Christian practices such as the Lord's Supper and baptism by immersion. But they also have special ceremonies in temples where believers are baptized for their ancestors and where families are united for eternity. The church is led by a man they consider to be a prophet, along with twelve apostles; local leaders are drawn from congregations to serve without pay for a limited period of time. The church sends missionaries two-by-two all over the world to preach their restored Christianity.

Illustration: The LDS temple in Salt Lake City, Utah; sego lilies are the state flowers of Utah; the sun, moon, and stars represent three tiers of heaven; the beehives suggest industry; the angels sounding the word of God, the all-seeing eye, and the words "Holiness to the Lord" appear on the temple.

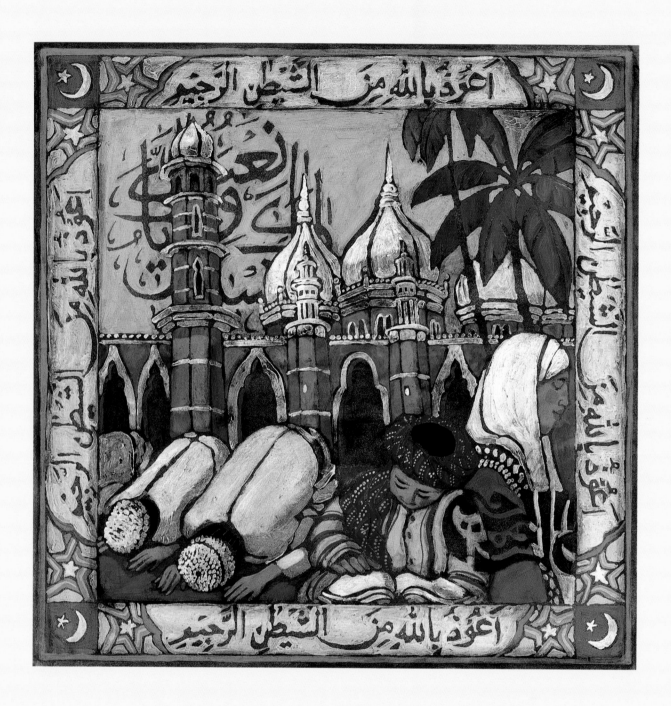

Muslims

When the prophet Abraham and his wife, Sarah, could not have children, God told Abraham to take a second wife, Hagar, Sarah's companion. She had a son, Ishmael. Later God commanded Abraham to take Hagar and her baby to the desert and leave them there. Abraham obeyed. In the desert, Hagar ran from one hill to another seven times looking for water while Ishmael cried and kicked the ground. According to tradition, water suddenly bubbled up where the baby's feet had touched the sand. The miraculous well became a sacred spot and later part of the city of Makkah (Mecca). It is near where Muslims believe that Abraham and Ishmael built the first house of worship to God, known as the Ka'bah. Centuries later, Muhammad, a merchant in Makkah, was troubled by the worship of idols. He spent hours praying in a cave when the Angel Gabriel appeared to him with the message that there is only one Creator God, called "Allah" in Arabic. Then the angel gave Muhammad other messages to share with the world.

Those who believe in one God and in Muhammad as his last prophet are called Muslims, and their religion is Islam, which means "peaceful submission" to God. The divine revelations to the prophet were recorded and together constitute the Qu'ran, Islam's holy scripture. Muslims pray at least five times a day. They give to the poor, fast from sunrise to sunset during the holy month of Ramadan, and they travel to Mecca at least once in their lives to encircle the shrine of Abraham. Muslims believe if they fulfill these duties faithfully, they will have walked a straight and holy path.

Illustration: The Masjid Jamek, in Kuala Lumpur, Malaysia; the decorative writing in the background is from the Qu'ran: "O, Lord, we only worship thee and thus seek your guidance and help." The writing to the right says, "I begin with the name of my Lord most merciful and beneficent," and in the border, "I seek protection from my creator against Satan the Cursed."

33.

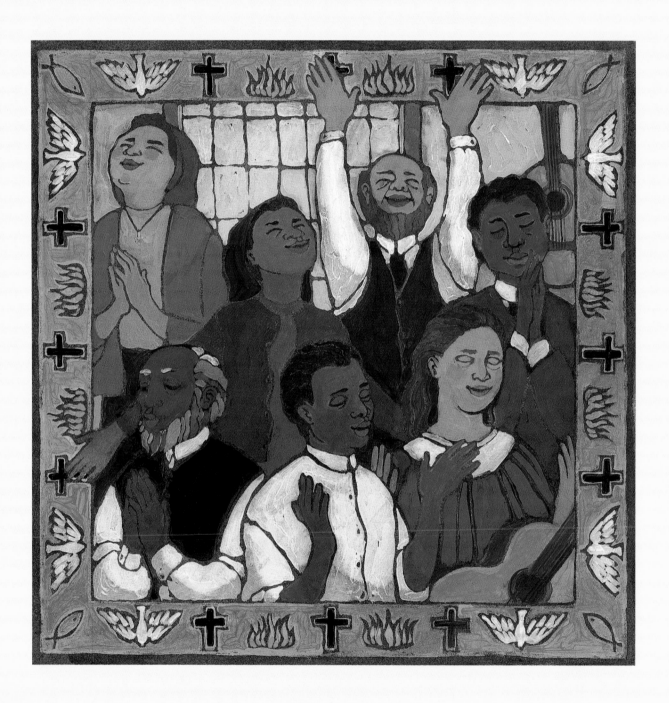

Pentecostals

One foggy evening in the spring of 1906, a group of Christians met in a Los Angeles warehouse to worship and pray. As Reverend William J. Seymour was preaching, strange, unfamiliar sounds came out of his mouth. He was "speaking in tongues"—speaking in a sort of divine language. His body was shaking with the power of the new sounds. Soon other people were doing the same thing. The whole building seemed to rock. Every day for the next three years, from early morning until midnight, thousands flocked to the warehouse on Azusa Street seeking the Holy Spirit. Pentecostalism had begun.

"Pentecost" means fifty and refers to a New Testament experience fifty days after Christ's resurrection when his apostles met together and were filled with the Holy Spirit. Pentecostals believe that each new Christian shows two signs of conversion: baptism in water and baptism by the Holy Spirit. Pentecostals can be healed by the Holy Spirit through their faith. In Sunday services believers sway to music, arms raised above their heads, as if calling on God to enter their bodies. Sometimes the languages they speak seem real, but most often no one on Earth has ever heard the sounds before. Pentecostals seek complete openness to an outpouring of God's spirit.

Illustration: The flying dove and the fire represent the Holy Spirit; the cross symbolizes Jesus' death; the fish represents Christ.

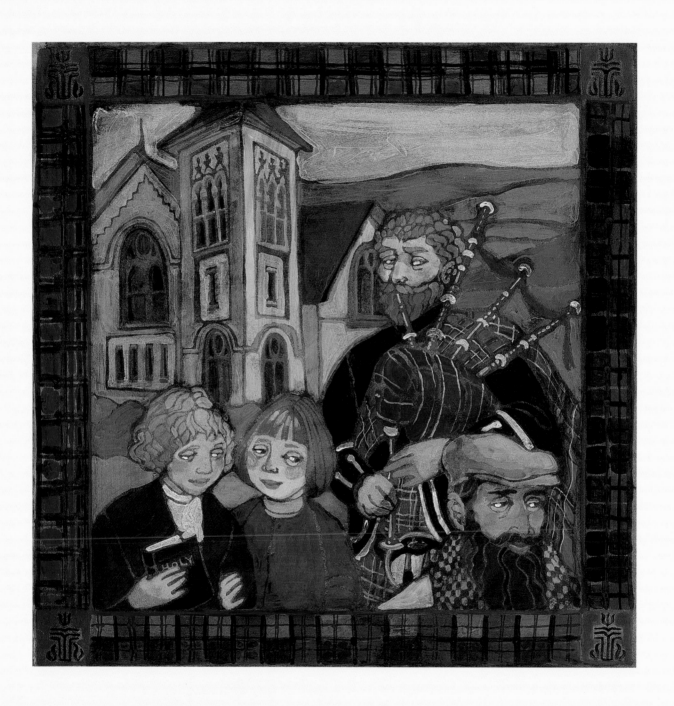

Presbyterians

John Calvin, a sixteenth-century French-Swiss lawyer, thought of God as the supreme judge—wise, powerful, and loving. This mighty God knows all things, including who the real believers are, Calvin taught, and God's will is expressed in the scriptures. Calvin rejected all Catholic traditions that were not mentioned in the Bible—saints, pilgrimages, and certain prayers. He believed that churches should be led not by a pope or bishop but by a group of church members known as "presbyters" or elders. John Knox, a devoted follower of Calvin, brought his ideas to Scotland where he convinced Mary, Queen of Scots, to declare Presbyterianism the state religion in 1560.

When they came to America, Presbyterians were among the strongest supporters of the Revolutionary War. Their form of church government influenced the new country's ideas of democracy. They believed that everyone should have a say in governing the church and the country. They believed strongly in learning, establishing more than seventy colleges and universities, including Princeton. Like many other Protestants, Presbyterians baptize infants and celebrate the Lord's Supper monthly. They try to balance the roles of ministers and members. God rules the universe, they assert, with all the faithful as his humble, and equal, servants.

Illustration: The Third Presbyterian Church in Salt Lake City, Utah; the tartan plaids of Scotland remind people of the church's beginnings; the symbol of the Presbyterian Church (USA) is in the corners.

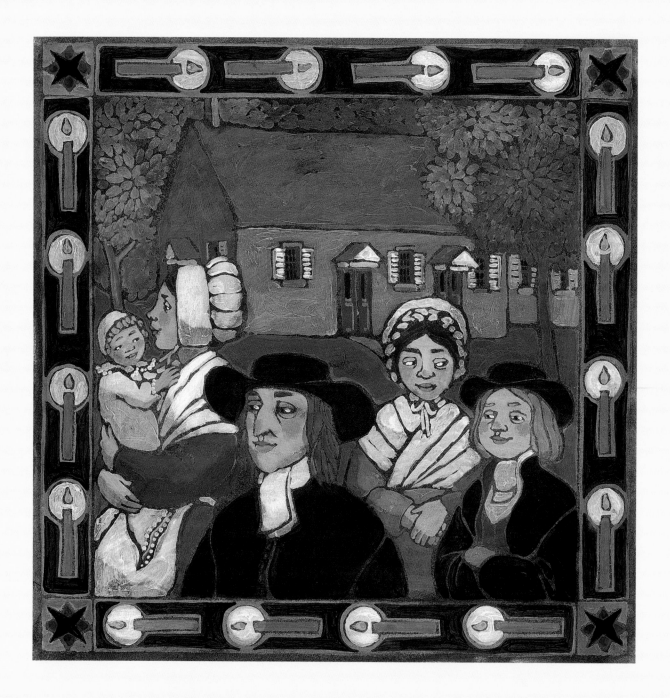

Quakers

George Fox felt he could not find truth in the seventeeth-century English churches. The sermons and the ceremonies were not enough for him. While praying one day, he heard a voice tell him that Truth is inside every human being. This Inner Light can be reached through prayer and meditation. With this new insight, Fox preached equality between men and women, rich and poor, slaves and free. Fox refused to take off his hat to royalty or to support clergy. Though they called themselves "The Religious Society of Friends," Fox's followers were nicknamed Quakers for saying that human beings would tremble—or quake—in God's presence. The Quakers were constantly persecuted—several were even hanged—before they found havens in New Jersey and Pennsylvania.

Quakers oppose war and shun oaths. Their buildings are simple, without paintings or organs or pulpits. During services, believers wait in silence until the Holy Spirit moves them to speak. Many congregations, called "meetings," have no paid clergy because they believe that all members are ministers. No special ceremonies such as baptism or the Lord's Supper are used. Quakers cherish the Bible for its truth, but they also believe that God communicates with human beings through divine revelation or the Inner Light.

Illustration: A Friends' meetinghouse in Birmingham, Pennsylvania, in 1763; the candle represents the inner light in each person; the star is the black and red star of the American Friends' Service; George Fox is in the center of the illustration.

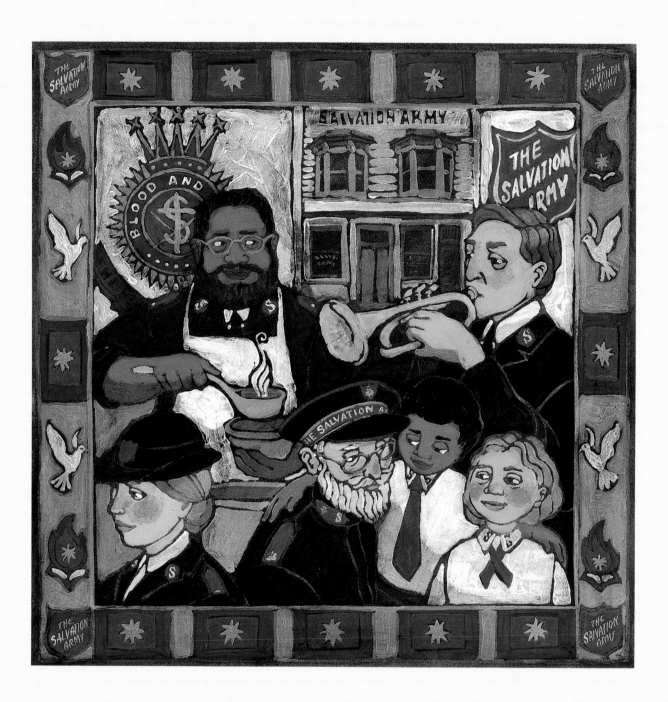

salvation Army

William Booth was leading a Christian mission among London's poor in the 1860s and feeling discouraged. Faith was not enough, he felt. His converts needed to get to work. But what would rally them? One day a church member called the group "God's volunteer army." Booth replied, "We're not volunteers. We are always on duty." In that moment, he decided to rename the mission "the Salvation Army." Almost immediately the group came alive. Modeled after the military, ministers became officers, congregations were corps, and members were transformed into soldiers. They donned uniforms, took up bugles, and marched against hunger and suffering with the motto: "Soap, soup, and salvation."

Salvationists meet weekly to worship in any available building. Officer (minister) candidates, both men and women, must be between eighteen and thirty-five years old with at least two years of formal Bible study. Men and women have been equal partners in leading the Army since the beginning. Uniformed officers can often be seen on street corners at Christmas carrying red kettles and ringing bells while collecting money for the poor. Sin destroys the soul and the society, they believe. But Jesus—with the help of the Army—can save everyone.

Illustration: A corps building in Dawson City, British Columbia, Canada, built in 1900; the shield suggests protection against sin; the crest says "blood and fire" to preach the gospel.

41.

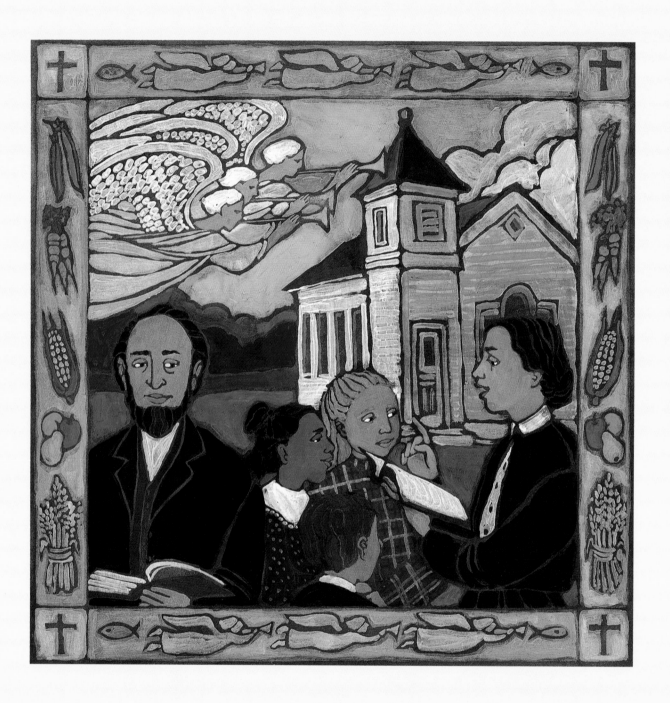

seventh-day Adventists

On the evening of October 22, 1844, seventeen-year-old Ellen White was among thousands of people waiting on rooftops and in churches to see Jesus. William Miller, a farmer who had studied the Bible, predicted that it would be the day of Christ's second coming. When nothing happened, most people went home, calling the day "The Great Disappointment." Ellen, a frail young girl, continued to meet with a small group of people who were trying to understand what went wrong. They concluded that instead of coming to earth, Christ had moved into the Most Holy Place in heaven for the next stage of his ministry. This was the beginning of the world's preparations for Jesus, and Ellen was to be one of God's messengers.

The name "Seventh-day Adventist" contains two of the church's beliefs. The word "advent" means "to come" and refers to Christ's return; the "seventh day," or Saturday, is when they celebrate the sabbath, instead of Sunday. Adventists emphasize good health and do not drink alcohol or smoke, and many are vegetarians. They believe in baptism by immersion for those who have reached an understanding of their commitment to Christ. Adventists educate their youth in their own schools and send out missionaries from their Maryland headquarters to prepare the world for the Second Coming.

Illustration: An Adventist church in Jackson, Mississippi; the fruits, vegetables, and grains represent the ethic of health; the three angels symbolize the second coming of Jesus; Ellen White is seen in the lower right.

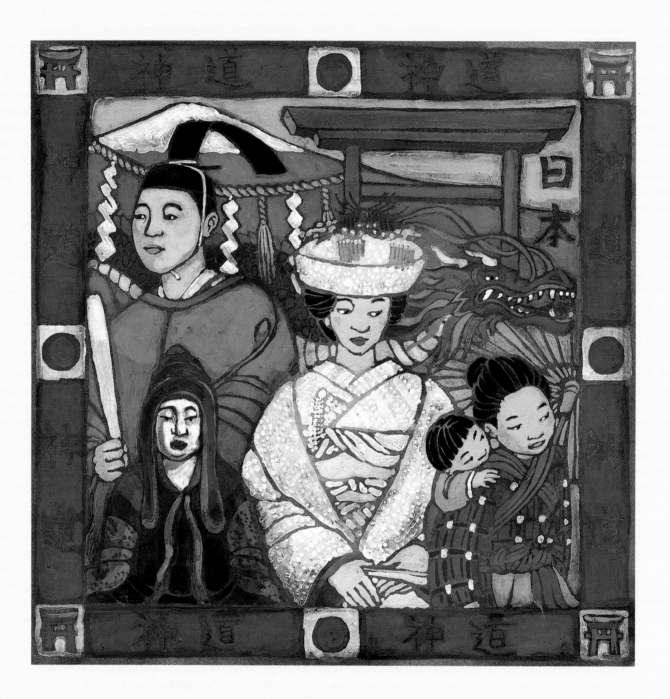

shintoists

In the beginning of time, the world was a large egg, which then divided into many separate pieces. The people of Japan believed that there were shadowy figures called "kami," or gods, who lived in the heavens and the earth. The kami had supernatural powers to bless human lives, but it was important not to displease them. So people made offerings to the gods in exchange for their help against disasters. Eventually the Japanese came to believe that their emperor was descended from the sun god and was to be worshipped and protected. Thousands of shrines were built, honoring the various kami and the emperor. After Japan was defeated in World War II, however, the people stopped worshipping the emperor and made Shinto a religion of the people.

Shinto, which means "way of the gods," teaches followers to care more about this world than about what lies beyond. Shinto priests bless crops and markets. Kami can also be worshipped in the home with food offerings such as rice, salt, and wine. Believers have ceremonies for certain times of life: birth, growing up, and marriage, as well as for the harvest, which often includes cleansing rituals. At several all-day shrine festivals, people celebrate together until a small portable shrine, carried on the shoulders of a group of men, passes by to bless their households. Shinto beliefs help people of Japan stay focused on this life and all its goodness.

Illustration: The torii, or gateway to the sacred space (two columns crossed by two beams); Mt. Fuji, Japan, is in the background; the sun represents the beginning of life in Japan; the thick rope of shimenawa suggests the sacred; the length of folded paper is the resting place of gods during prayer.

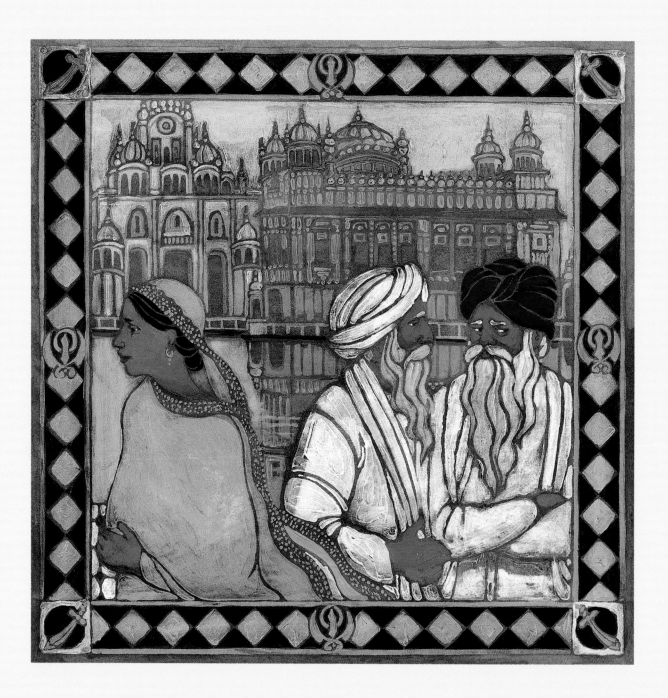

sikhs

In India during the late fifteenth century, a young man named Guru Nanak was troubled by the fighting between Muslims, who believed in one God, and Hindus, who taught that God takes many forms. While pondering these claims, Nanak disappeared and didn't return for three days. He was summoned into God's presence, Sikhs believe, where he learned that there is only one truth: universal love. Nanak's insight was passed down through the generations by nine successive gurus, or spiritual leaders and teachers. Two hundred years after Nanak, the Sikhs—meaning disciples—formed a society of holy men and soldiers to defend their faith. This group, called khalsa, developed five outward signs of their loyalty: uncut hair covered with a turban, a comb to hold the hair, a dagger, a steel wristband, and short trousers. Soon all male Sikhs adopted the five signs. Later, females were invited to join the khalsa.

God is not revealed in religious ceremonies but in quiet prayer and with the help of gurus, say the Sikhs. God himself is a guru. Sikhs say five different prayers a day, each one written by a different guru. Boys and girls become members of the khalsa at fourteen, or whenever they feel ready. Believers avoid alcohol and tobacco. They encourage hospitality to strangers, so Sikh temples have kitchens for hungry visitors and rooms where travelers can sleep. In the temples, believers sing hymns to God and read from their holy scripture, the Sri Guru Granth Sahib, which is the spiritual poetry of all God's teachers.

Illustration: The Golden Temple in the Pool of Immortality in Amritsar, India; a sword is one of the five symbols of Sikh faith; the diamond pattern imitates the tiles of the plaza.

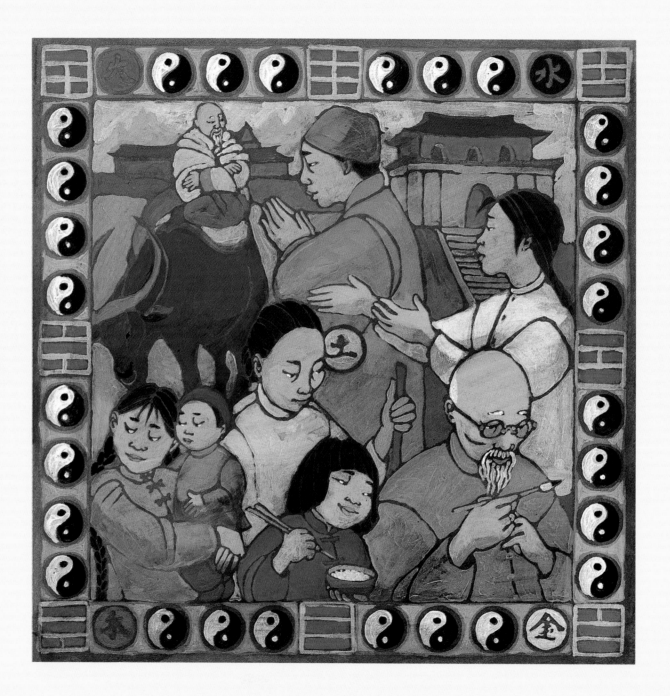

Taoists

It is said that Lao-tzu, a Chinese librarian, was disgusted with the foolishness at the Emperor's Court around 600 B.C. and left for the countryside. As he reached the city's gates, the guards begged Lao-tzu to tell all that he had learned. His words became the Tao Te Ching, a book of wisdom. Lao-tzu taught that the world is made of an unchanging essence known as the Tao. From the Tao—meaning the Way—come two opposite forces known as the yin and the yang, he said. All of life is made of these opposites, day and night, life and death, man and woman. These opposites overlap each other, however. They come together and then separate eternally, creating life's many rhythms.

People who follow the Tao believe the vital energy inside every living thing—called "ch'i," meaning breath—holds the secret to everlasting life. They have daily breathing exercises based on the movements of cranes and tortoises which are believed to have long life. Religious Taoists also believe the world is populated with magical spirits. It is the role of priests to manage these spirits so that worshippers can be healed, purified, and made whole. These priests perform many ceremonies to help believers regain harmony with nature and themselves. The power of the Tao draws people toward quiet self-forgetfulness.

Illustration: Taishan, on Mt. Tai, China, is the most famous mountain shrine; the eight trigrams are used with the Taoist writings; the five elements or forces of nature are suggested by different colors: fire is red, water is black, earth is yellow, wood is green, and metal is white.

49.

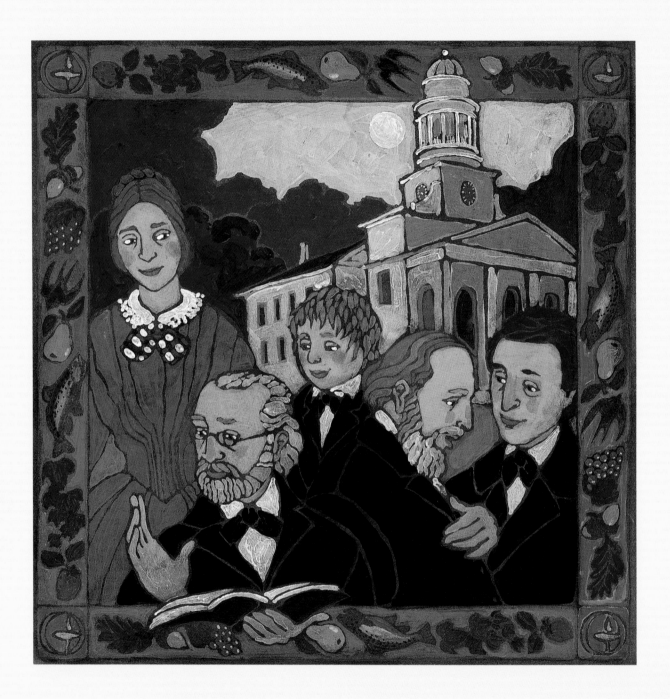

unitarians

When William Ellery Channing stood up to preach one wintry day in 1819, his hands were shaking but his voice was calm. For the last few years, people in New England had been arguing about whether Jesus was God and how much humans had to rely on God. Channing told the congregation that Jesus was a prophetic teacher with a spark of divinity in him but was not God. All people have the same spark, he said. He urged his listeners to look for God inside themselves. Channing was the first to use the word "Unitarian," meaning "one," rather than the traditional Trinity, or "three," referring to the Father, Son, and Holy Spirit. Though many people rejected Channing's ideas at first, eventually many of Massachusetts's oldest churches converted to Unitarianism.

Unitarians, who merged with the Universalists in 1961, emphasize the importance of the mind and education. They believe people need to find their own paths to God. They also believe in the goodness of the earth and all its inhabitants. All people are important and should be treated fairly and kindly. The Bible is only one source of truth among many, they say. Most Unitarians have no official religious ceremonies or prescribed doctrines but direct their energies toward establishing peace and justice in the world.

Illustration: The First Church of Christ, Unitarian, in Lancaster, Massachusetts; each element represents nature and strong ties to the natural world; the flaming chalice symbolizes the warmth of community as the fire of creative truth drawn from an eternal cup; the two circles represent the joining of Unitarianism and Universalism.

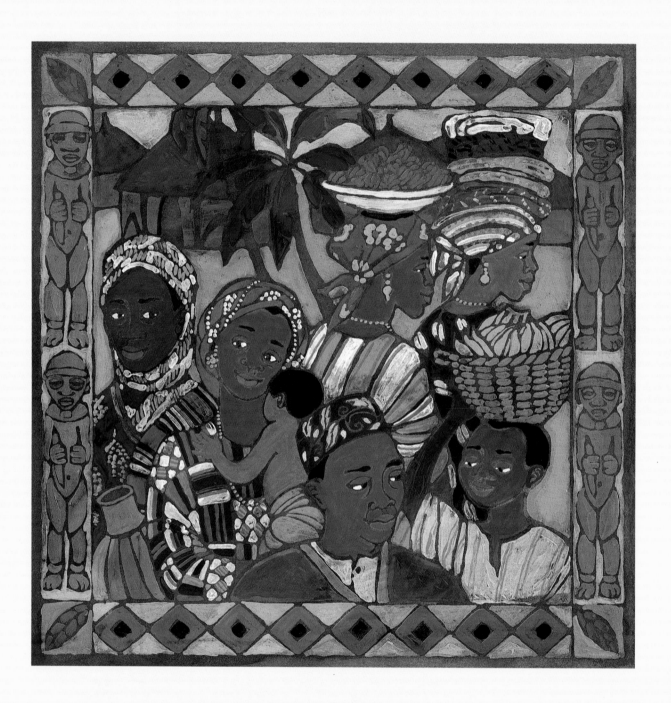

yorubas

The world was once nothing but a sea of lava, said the Yorubas, an ancient tribe living along the Niger River in Africa. So God sent spirits—orishas—to create dry land. The orishas descended to earth on a gold chain. They shaped the rivers, hills, trees, flowers, and birds. After they finished, the spirits entered their creations, making all things alive. Then God breathed life into human beings. Evil spirits began to battle good spirits. The only way to make peace was to offer a sacrifice—perhaps fruit, flowers, candles, or favorite foods. For life's biggest problems, Yorubas sacrificed animals. Beginning in the seventeenth century, Yorubas were brought to America as slaves. In Cuba their religion mixed with Catholicism, and orishas were viewed as saints. This new faith was called Santeria, or "the worship of saints."

Yorubas believe that good behavior helps keep a balance among the spirits. Family members who have died return often to make sure that the living are being good. People seek the help of priests and priestesses to heal the sick and restore harmony. They contact the spirits through dancing. Sometimes they believe the spirits enter human bodies. Many Yorubas now are Muslims or Christians, but underneath they continue to believe in orishas who fight and dance and help needy humans.

Illustration: Rural huts in Africa; weaving; carvings used in ancestor worship.

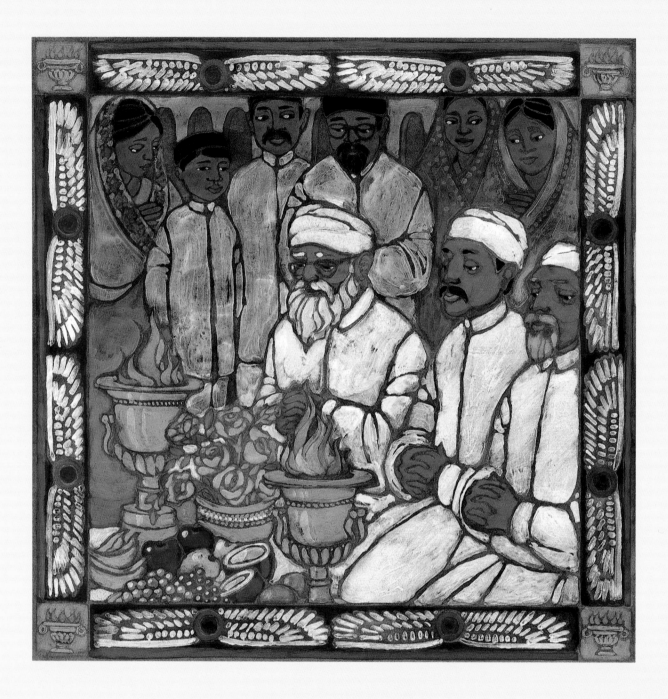

zoroastrians

A long time before Muhammad, Jesus, or even Buddha, the prophet Zoroaster lived in Persia (now Iran). He had many visions in which he learned that the world is ruled by one supreme god, Ahura Mazda, who is in an eternal battle with an evil power called Angra Mainya. Ahura Mazda created the world and human beings to help him in the struggle. People must choose whom to follow. Goodness will triumph, Zoroaster taught, when people follow the three-fold path of good thoughts, good works, and good deeds. After death, each soul will cross a bridge that widens to help righteous people in their journey toward heaven but becomes razor-thin for the wicked, causing them to drop into a dark pit.

Fire represents God and truth, Zoroastrians (or Parsis, as they are called now) believe, and so a fire burns in their temples at all times. They pray five times each day, facing the light. At age seven, boys and girls receive a white undershirt to wear the rest of their lives as a sign of faith. They also get a sacred cord which is wrapped around their waist three times, reminding them of their connection to God. At marriage, a priest uses a similar cord to encircle the couple, symbolizing their unity. With these symbolic acts, Zoroastrians show their love of God and their willingness to fight against evil.

Illustration: Light symbolizes righteousness; wings represent the divinity that exists in every person; fire symbolizes God and truth.

the golden rule

as taught in many traditions

Baha'i

"Ascribe not to any soul that which thou wouldst not have ascribed to thee,
and say not that which thou doest not." —Bahá'u'lláh

Hidden Words, Arabic 29

Buddhism

"Just as you did for yourself, likewise do the same for others too." —Buddha

Udānavarga 23:8

Christianity

"Do unto others as you would have them do unto you." —Jesus

The Bible, Luke 6:31

Confucianism

"Do not do to others what you do not want done to yourself." —Confucius

The Analects 15:23

Hinduism

"Do not to others what ye do not wish done to yourself. This is the whole
Dharma; heed it well." —Sage Vyasa

The Mahābhārata 5:1517

56.

Islam

"No one of you is a believer until you desire for another that which
you desire for yourself." —Muhammad

An-Nawawi, Hadīth 13

Judaism

"What is hateful to you, do not do to your neighbor. That is the entire Torah;
the rest is commentary." —Rabbi Hillel

Babylonian Talmud, Shabbat 31a

Native American

"Respect for all life is the foundation." —Deganawidah

The Great Law of Peace

Sikhism

"Be not estranged from another, for in every heart pervades
the Lord." —Guru Arjan Dev

Sri Guru Granth Sahib

Zoroastrianism

"Human nature is good only when it does not do unto another whatever
is not good for its own self." —Manuskihar

Dādistān-ī-Dīnīk 94:5

Our thanks to Professor Dorothy Marcic of Vanderbilt University for bringing these quotations to our attention. They are in her book, *Managing with the Wisdom of Love: Uncovering Virtue in People and Organizations*, published by Jossey-Bass.

Peggy Fletcher Stack was born and raised in New Jersey, studied at the Graduate Theological Union in Berkeley, California, traveled through Africa with her news-photographer husband, and worked at *Books and Religion* in Manhattan before settling down as a religion writer at the *Salt Lake Tribune*. She currently serves on the advisory board of PBS's "Religion and Ethics News Weekly." She and her husband have three children.

———

Kathleen Peterson was born in the Rocky Mountains and has lived in Hawaii and Malaysia and painted in Central America, Nepal, and Thailand. She is the illustrator of *The Lesson* and *Stones of the Temple*, among other books. Currently she is the director of the Central Utah Art Center, and each summer she and her husband run the Bennion Teton Boys Ranch in Idaho. They have four children.

"*A World of Faith* is an important book—a creative introduction to the great diversity of faith in our nation, which will help children view their world more openly. As president of NCCJ, an organization dedicated for over seventy years to fighting prejudice and promoting mutual respect among all, I am convinced that young readers of this book will look back years later and realize it was one of those critical first steps leading them to the path of greater interfaith understanding."

SANFORD CLOUD, JR.
President, National Conference for Community and Justice